I dedicate this book to my father,
Ernani Vilela,
who never loved soccer,
but taught me to see the art
behind every detail of life.
—C. V.

Henry Holt and Company, LLC
Publishers since 1866
175 Fifth Avenue
New York, New York 10010
mackids.com

Library of Congress Cataloging-in-Publication Data is available.

ISBN 978-1-62779-123-6

Henry Holt books may be purchased for business or promotional use. For information
on bulk purchases, please contact Macmillan Corporate and Premium Sales Department at
(800) 221-7945 x5442 or by e-mail at specialmarkets@macmillan.com.

First American edition—2014

Printed in China by Toppan Leefung Printing, Dongguan City, Guangdong Province.

10 9 8 7 6 5 4 3 2 1

GOAL!

Written by **Sean Taylor**

Photographs by **Caio Vilela**

Henry Holt and Company
New York

Where there's a ball, there will always be someone who wants to play soccer.

Brazil

Many people say the Brazilian player Pelé was the greatest soccer player ever. He helped Brazil win three World Cups and was so admired that he once stopped a war. In 1967, his team, Santos, traveled to Nigeria to play a game. Nigeria was in the middle of a war, but the armies agreed to stop fighting so that they could see Pelé play.

When you play soccer, you're not allowed to use your arms and hands unless you are the goalkeeper.

But you can use the rest of your body— your feet, your legs, your hips, your chest, and your head.

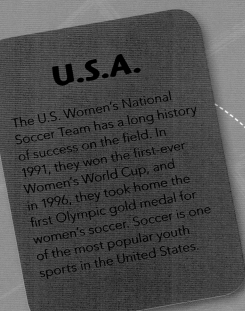

U.S.A.

The U.S. Women's National Soccer Team has a long history of success on the field. In 1991, they won the first-ever Women's World Cup, and in 1996, they took home the first Olympic gold medal for women's soccer. Soccer is one of the most popular youth sports in the United States.

There are more than 6,000 different languages spoken on our planet. But children all over the world understand soccer.

Spain

In Spain, a soccer ball is called el balón de fútbol. Before a soccer ball can be used in the FIFA World Cup, it must first be weighed three times in a sealed cabinet in a laboratory to make sure that it is within the approved limits. FIFA allows balls between 14.8 and 15.7 ounces (420 and 445 grams) for use.

In some sports, teams can score up to 100 points in a game.

In a soccer game you don't get many goals. Sometimes you don't get any at all. You have to be patient. So when a goal comes, it's special!

England

England was one of the first countries to form a national soccer team. In 1863, a group of Englishmen met in London and formed the Football Association, which still runs English soccer today. They established the rules of the modern game. But games similar to soccer are known to have been played thousands of years ago in China, Greece, the Roman Empire, and Japan.

When the ball comes your way,
you might feel excited, you might feel calm,
you might even feel a bit scared.

Playing soccer teaches you lots of things—
how to be quick, how to be clever,
how to see what's going on around you,
and how to be brave.

You can play soccer almost anywhere—
in a garden, down an alley, on a playground,
in a park, or on a beach.

Togo

The men's national soccer team in Togo is called the Sparrow Hawks. On May 6, 2001, a teenager from Togo became the youngest person to play in a World Cup qualifier. Souleymane Mamam represented Togo in a game against Zambia when he was just 13 years old.

You don't need to buy anything
to play soccer. You can make goalposts
with two stones, two sticks, or two shirts.

If you don't have a real soccer ball, you can make
one with rolled-up socks, newspaper and string,
or even an orange in a plastic bag.

Tanzania

On July 2, 2013, Tanzania President Jakaya Kikwete and U.S. President Barack Obama tested a very special soccer ball. Called the Soccket, this soccer ball can bring power to people around the world. Designed to create, capture, and store energy, the Soccket soccer ball can be used to charge small electronics, such as cellphones and lamps.

Some people invent machines. Some people invent medicines. And some people invent tricks with soccer balls.

When you trick a defender by pretending to go one way and then send the player after an imaginary ball, it's called a step-over. When you throw yourself in the air and kick the ball over your head, it's called a bicycle kick.

Jordan

In a qualifying game for the 2013 Women's Asian Cup, the Jordan women's soccer team beat the Kuwait women's soccer team 21–0, advancing Jordan to their first-ever Asian Cup finals. One of their players, Maysa Jbarah, scored a hat-trick—she scored three goals—in an amazing three minutes.

Every soccer game is like a story.
It's full of characters, emotions, and drama.

And no one knows how it will end
until the final whistle blows.

Iran

The greatest goal scorer in international men's soccer is an Iranian player named Ali Daei. Between 1993 and 2006, he played in 149 games for Iran. He helped his country qualify for two World Cups and scored 109 goals. The next-highest international goal-scorer, Ferenc Puskás, scored only 84 goals for Hungary between 1945 and 1956.

There's nothing quite like the excitement before you start a game of soccer. Anything can happen!

Pakistan

The biggest sport in Pakistan is cricket, and soccer has not traditionally been as popular. But that may change. In 2011, Pakistan's men's Under-16 team won the South Asian Football Federation Championships.

At the end of the game, you may have won or you may have lost. But you can lose a game and still play your very best. And that is a kind of winning.

India

The highest-scoring game in the First Division of India's soccer league was played on May 30, 2011, when Dempo Sporting Club beat Air India 14–0. Ranti Martins broke the record for goals scored in one game—he hit the back of the net six times.

Soccer is not about showing off how well you can play. It's about showing how well you can play for your team.

The best players don't worry about being the stars of their teams. They want their teams to be the stars.

Nepal

Although it wasn't always the case, soccer is now a very popular sport in Nepal. In 2009, more than 10,000 people watched a charity game in Nepal between a team of politicians and a team of TV comedians. The comedians won 4–1.

The ball doesn't care if you're big or small.
It doesn't care what your religion is,
what race you are, or where you come from.
It doesn't even care if you're good at soccer.

Anyone can play soccer—anywhere in the world.

China

Jia you! means "go, team!" in Chinese. In the People's Republic of China, the women's national team was the runner-up in the 1996 Olympic Women's Soccer Final and in the 1999 Women's World Cup Final. The men's national team, nicknamed the Dragon or the Great Wall, won the East Asian Cup in 2005 and 2010.

You can have fun playing soccer with just one friend or even on your own.

Burma
(Myanmar)

For some time, Burma, officially known as Myanmar, had an unusual soccer league. All the teams in its top league were from the capital city, Rangoon, and most teams were run by different government departments. The premier club for many years was called Finance and Revenue!

No other sport brings people together like soccer. No other sport is played by so many people in so many different countries.

When you are playing soccer, there will always be someone else playing, somewhere in the world.

New Zealand

The New Zealand soccer team qualified for its first-ever World Cup in 1982. That same year, the players traveled a record total of 55,000 miles. And goalkeeper Richard Wilson managed nine clean sheets—nine shutouts—in a row.

Soccer Around the World

Soccer is played all over the world!
And in most other countries—except Canada
and the U.S.A.—it is called football.

Here are all the countries mentioned in this book and the
year each country's first national soccer team was founded.

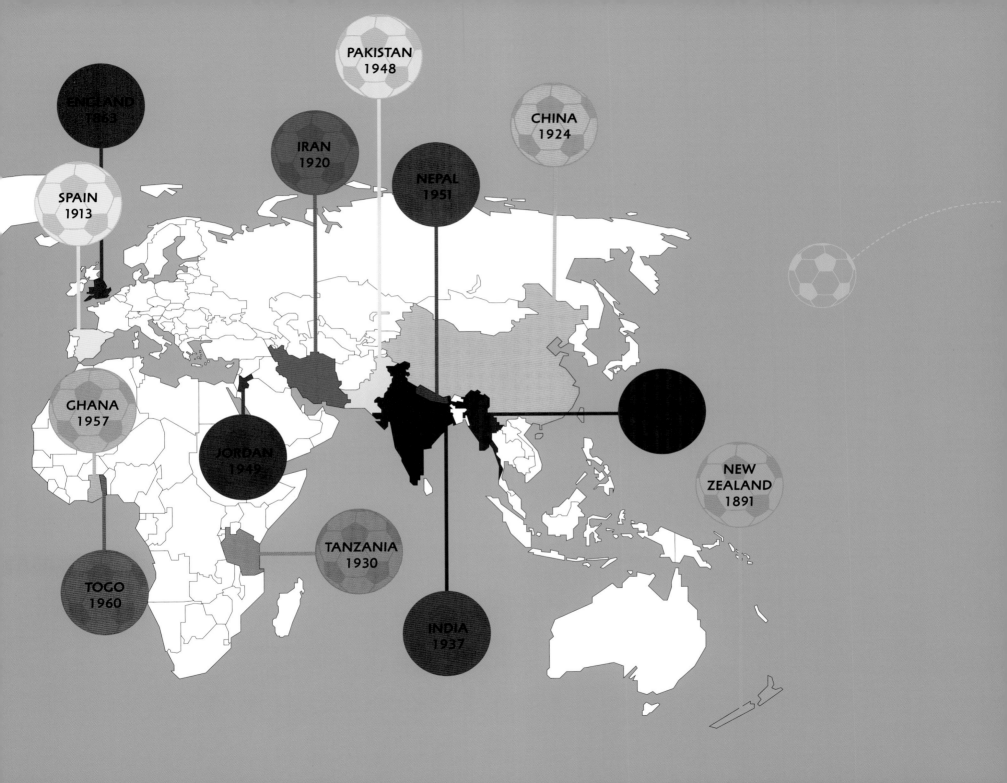